7 AMAZING POWERS OF YOUR TONGUE

MASTERING THE ARTS OF UTILIZING YOUR TONGUE'S INCREDIBLE ABILITIES

BY JOHN BAPTIST NATHAN

7 Amazing Powers of Your Tongue

Mastering the art of utilizing your tongue's incredible abilities

By

John Baptist Nathan

information, products, services, or opinions contained within that material. The use of third-party material does not guarantee that your results will mirror our results.

The publication of such third-party material is simply a recommendation and expression of the author's own opinion of that material. Whether due to the progression of the Internet or unforeseen changes in company policy and editorial submission guidelines, what is stated as fact at the time of this writing may become outdated or inapplicable later.

ABOUT THE AUTHOR

Greetings, esteemed readers! I am John Baptist Nathan, the proud founder of the Be Blessed Academy and the author of this remarkable book.

Beyond my role as an author, I also serve as a life coach, an approved counselor, and a certified career analyst. Throughout my journey, I have encountered countless individuals facing various challenges in life, relationships, and careers. I am genuinely thankful to the Divine for allowing me to assist people from around the globe in different aspects of their lives.

In my preaching, teaching, and coaching endeavors, I have gained invaluable insights. Among these treasures of knowledge, one particular revelation has led to the creation of this beautiful book.

Congratulations on acquiring this literary gem, for it holds the key to unlocking the power of your words and fostering personal growth and manifestation.

In the Book of John, Chapter 1:1, we find the profound words: "In the beginning was the Word, and the Word was with God, and the Word was God." This verse awakened me to our words' immense influence and their profound impact on our lives. Many of us remain oblivious to the power in our tongues, but fear not, for this book will enlighten you on its significance.

The tongue, often overlooked, is an extraordinary organ within our bodies. It enables us to taste, eat, and chew and also allows us to communicate and express ourselves. The little bumps adorning our tongues play a vital role in our sense of taste, allowing us to savor the flavors of our food.

Furthermore, the tongue is an incredibly versatile and handy muscle that allows us to articulate many words. This literary masterpiece will serve as your guide to unlocking the immense potential of your tongue and its ability to revolutionize your existence.

Lastly, I implore you to treat your tongue with utmost care and reverence. It is a precious gem nestled within your oral cavity, deserving unwavering attention.

Gratitude is extended to you for perusing this literary gem, and it is my sincerest wish that it aids you on your voyage of self-exploration and individual development.

TABLE OF CONTENTS

INTRODUCTION

We often overlook and rarely give much thought to our tongue, but it possesses a remarkable power to create and destroy. The tongue plays a crucial role in our lives through the spoken word, whether within our families, businesses, or nations. It is through our tongues our words are released, words that have the potential to either build up or tear down. The taste buds on our tongues, these tiny sensory organs, allow us to experience the many flavors surrounding us. They guide us in distinguishing between what is delicious and what is unpleasant.

Additionally, our taste buds serve as a warning system, alerting us to spoiled milk or rotten meat while we eat. Beyond its sensory function, the tongue also contributes to the richness and romance of our lives. We can express our deepest emotions and desires with our tongues.

Even when we fall ill, the doctor examines our tongue. Remember those doctor visits when they would shine a light in your mouth and say, "Open wide"? It's interesting to think about the power of our words and how they can impact our lives. Affirmations, positive and uplifting language, motivational speeches, life coaching, counseling, preaching, and teaching all rely on the power of our words. Can you imagine using the power of affirmation or motivating others without using our tongues? It's impossible.

We often need to pay more attention to just how much we talk. On average, people speak around 150 words per minute. There is no substantial evidence to suggest that women talk more than men. Studies show that an average person speaks around 16,000 words daily, but we probably say even more. Every single word we speak requires the use of our tongue, so imagine the importance of this small organ in allowing us to communicate with such volume.

Our tongues are vital in our lives, yet we rarely give them much thought or attention. We need to learn about the incredible organ that enables us to speak. It's been said that words hurt more than physical punches, and I'm sure many of us can attest to the truth of this statement based on personal experience. While physical wounds may fade with time, the impact of hurtful words can linger indefinitely. We remember the words that cut us deeply and the pain we felt upon hearing them. Not only do we experience hurt, but we also have the power to inflict it upon others.

Words possess the incredible power to affect us profoundly. Hurtful words can cause emotional pain that lasts far longer than physical pain. Verbal abuse, insults, and derogatory remarks can leave lasting scars on our self-esteem and mental well-being. Unlike physical wounds, emotional wounds caused by hurtful words can be more complex to heal. It is essential for us to recognize the weight our words carry and to use them responsibly, with kindness and empathy.

I have found myself speaking disrespectfully towards my mother numerous times, unaware of the potential hurt my words may have caused her. The power of words is truly remarkable, as they possess the ability to bring about positive outcomes. Unfortunately, succumbing to the temptation of uttering mean-spirited and hurtful remarks is too easy simply because they may seem amusing or grant us a false sense of authority.

Our emotions often overshadow our better judgment, much like a small rudder that steers an entire ship. In this book, I have outlined seven remarkable capabilities of the human tongue.

These seven unique ways of utilizing our speech hold great significance. Regrettably, I have neglected to guide how to employ these abilities effectively. However, upon reading this book, you will learn the art of utilizing your tongue in a powerful, uplifting, and empathetic manner.

Chapter 1

The Incredible Power of Dead Words

There is no worse death than the end of hope – Pelagius

Synopsys

This chapter unfolds the destructive power of words, using real-life examples and biblical narratives to illustrate how spoken words can lead to significant loss in businesses, relationships, and personal development. Through compelling stories, it emphasizes the lasting impact of "dead words" and the challenge of undoing their damage.

Power of Dead Words

I am delighted to discover that one of the incredible powers of the tongue is its ability to cause harm and loss.

The tongue is a highly influential part of our bodies. When used carelessly, it can inflict significant damage. Words discouraging and demoralizing are considered "dead words" because they hinder growth and productivity.

Let me share a real story to illustrate this power. A man had been selling burgers for many years and earning a good income. He sent his son to a prestigious university to study Business Management with his earnings. After his son graduated, he returned and warned his father about an upcoming recession affecting the nation. Trusting his son's expertise, the father believed him.

As a result, the burger business slowed down, and people stopped buying burgers from his shop. Eventually, the father completely shut down his burger business despite its previous success. It was the words spoken by his son that brought about this loss.

This incident demonstrates how the tongue can cause loss in businesses, relationships, careers, and organizations.

The Holy Bible has a powerful story about Jesus that teaches us about the power of our words. Jesus and His disciples were on their way to Bethany when Jesus saw a fig tree with leaves but no fruit. He cursed the tree, saying, "May no one ever eat fruit from you again." The disciples heard this, and the next day, they witnessed the tree withering from the roots. Jesus knew the power of His words and explained to His disciples that they also possessed the same power.

We often underestimate the power of our words. We may not perform miracles like Jesus, but we frequently speak words of loss, unproductivity, fear, and hatred. These "dead words" can have a destructive impact on others.

Let me share another story to illustrate this. There was a boy who had a quick temper and often spoke rudely to people. His father instructed him to hammer a nail into a fence whenever he felt angry or rude.

On the first day, he hammered in 37 nails. He hammered in fewer nails as he learned to control his anger and rudeness. His father then told him that if he could stay calm, he could remove any nail he didn't hammer that day. When he pulled out the nails, he saw the holes left behind. His father explained that those holes represented the pain caused by his rudeness. While the pain may fade over time, the impact of his words remained.

Just as it is impossible to put toothpaste back into the tube, once "dead words" leave our mouths, taking them back or forgetting them is challenging. These words can destroy relationships, homes, and even lives. They can stay with a person for a lifetime.

Children are particularly vulnerable to the negative words of their parents, which can harm their spirit and future. Criticism, blame, and unpleasant comments from a spouse can drain the spirit, affecting their career and relationship.

Any word that instills a sense of loss is considered a "dead word." If a word causes someone to lose confidence, courage, hope, or commitment, it is considered dead because it hampers their productivity. Being unproductive is a detrimental state in itself.

Wrapping up

Remember: words have power. They can either build or destroy. The stories shared highlight the lasting impact of negative words and the challenge of undoing their harm.

Let's choose our words wisely, aiming to uplift and inspire as we delve into strategies for positive communication in the upcoming chapters.

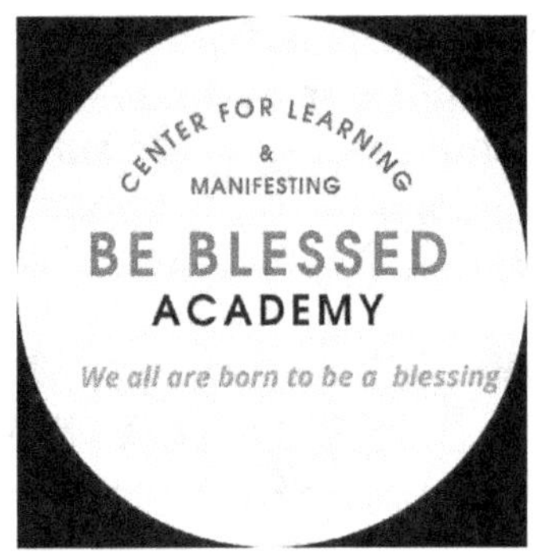

Chapter 2

The Incredible Power of Life-Giving Words

Nothing is more appealing than speaking

Beautiful, life giving word- Proverbs 16:24

Synopsys

Discover the transformative power of life-giving words. Contrasting with the previous focus on dead words, the narrative introduces the idea that our speech has the ability to bring positive change and abundance. Through the story of a hunchbacked King, readers witness the profound impact of life-giving words and are encouraged to reflect on their own moments of positive speech.

Power of Life-Giving Words

I am thrilled to share with you the profound realization that our words possess an extraordinary ability to bring forth life. Yes, you heard it right - our tongues hold the power to both give life and bring death.

This captivating chapter will delve into using our tongues to release life-giving words. But let me clarify: we are not merely talking about positive words but words that can produce goodness and blessings in our lives.

In the previous chapter, we explored the concept of dead words - those that are unproductive and bear no fruit. Now, we shall focus on the life-giving words. These words can bring about positive change and abundance in our lives. However, more is needed to learn how to speak life-giving words; we must also understand how to communicate them effectively.

Before we proceed any further, please take a few moments to reflect on the last time you spoke words that you believed brought about positive outcomes for yourself or others. Allow yourself to bask in the memory of those moments, for they hold the key to unlocking the potential within your words.

Now, let me share with you a captivating story. Once upon a time, there was a hunchbacked King who was deeply dissatisfied with his condition. Despite his efforts to find a cure, he was met with disappointment. A wise man visited the King one fateful day and conversed deeply. As their discussion drew close, the wise man humbly requested the King's permission to suggest his hunchbacked condition. Intrigued, the King granted his request.

The wise man shared his suggestion with the King and departed. Inspired by the wise man's words, the King summoned a sculptor to his presence. He instructed the sculptor to create a stone statue of himself but with one crucial difference - the statue should stand tall and straight, devoid of any hunch. The sculptor understood the King's wishes and crafted a magnificent statue that portrayed the King in all his regal splendor, standing upright.

The statue was placed in the palace garden for all to see. The sight of the statue left the palace inhabitants astounded and filled with curiosity. They marveled at the resemblance between the statue and their hunchbacked King. However, they soon realized this statue was different - it stood tall and proud, unlike their King. The news of the statue spread like wildfire, and conversations buzzed throughout the palace.

The King would visit the garden every morning and evening, standing before the statue and contemplating its likeness. He would draw strength from this daily ritual, which became integral to his routine. Even the Queen, puzzled by the King's behavior, questioned him.

The King then revealed the wise man's suggestion - to place the straight statue and gaze upon it daily, believing that his hunchbacked condition would gradually disappear.

The words of the King's straight statue spread far and wide, capturing everyone's attention. The entire palace and village became aware of this miraculous transformation, and a grand celebration ensued. The hunchbacked King was finally freed from his condition, thanks to the life-giving words bestowed upon him by the wise man.

Of course, the King's actions and adherence to the wise man's advice brought about his healing. Nevertheless, the wise man's words ignited the spark of hope and initiated this incredible journey.

Let us take a moment to reflect on the power of our words. Imagine how our productive words could impact our children, spouses, parents, colleagues, friends, neighbors, and relatives. At the end of each day, before retiring to bed, I encourage you to record the productive words you have spoken. Maintaining a journal of these words will be a powerful reminder and inspire you to release even more life-giving words the following day.

If you have yet to speak life-giving words, I implore you to start today. Remember, you can speak life into existence through the power of your tongue. Embrace this incredible gift and let your words bring blessings and abundance to your life and those around you.

When we choose to use our words in a hostile and unproductive manner, we also have the power to use them positively and upliftingly. Often, in our quest to appear superior, knowledgeable, wise, and clever, we tend to belittle others by speaking unpleasant words. We train ourselves to always talk negatively by continuously engaging in such behavior.

We know that our thoughts shape our communication, but our words will be addressed with the ability to speak physically. This highlights the importance of our words.

However, we possess an incredible ability to speak words that bring life and encouragement. Consider the following phrases: "You can do it" - these simple words have the power to inspire and motivate both ourselves and others. Regardless of the situation, we can confidently declare, "Whatever it is, I will always find a solution."

Moreover, repeatedly affirming "It's done," we can expedite our progress and ultimately achieve our goals.

Isn't it Wonderful - repeating this word brings joy to your day?

Isn't it wonderful to know that she is making a recovery? Isn't it incredible to know that they have reconciled? Isn't it marvelous to see them happy and celebrating?

"I have faith that you will succeed"- when you say these words to someone going for an interview, exam, or competition, it brings them calmness and assurance.

"Fully Paid" is another influential phrase people can use when they have debts and are struggling to repay something. These are just a few examples of powerful words that you can incorporate into your daily life.

Start by speaking them to yourself; you can share them with others once you see positive results.

In my coaching, I provide my clients with Power Code Words tailored to their specific goals. For example, if they want to buy a house, I give 30 Power Codes that, when implemented, can bring about positive changes in their life. Many people have benefited and achieved great things by using these Power Codes.

It is important to speak words that give life and positivity, but often, we struggle to do so because of the negative thoughts and emotions in our minds and hearts.

What we fill our minds and hearts with will ultimately come out of our mouths. Therefore, before we can start filling our minds and hearts with good things, we need to ask ourselves how they became filled with negativity in the first place.

Our minds and hearts are influenced by what we hear. Children learn bad words by being exposed to them. We hear harmful words that become implanted in our minds and hearts. We absorb these words and then speak them ourselves. This cycle of hearing and speaking continues.

Let me share a secret: "You are the first person to hear what you speak." Whether or not anyone else hears you, you listen to yourself when you speak. So, to plant good things in your mind and heart, you need to start chatting life-giving words.

You can use your words to bring life and positivity to yourself and others. With time, these life-giving words will become ingrained in your mind and heart, and you won't have to try to speak them consciously; they will flow naturally.

These life-giving words are like positive affirmations and anchoring words that stabilize your mind and heart. An unstable mind is easily swayed and cannot achieve much, so it is essential to anchor your mind and heart with these positive words, especially during challenging situations.

Allow wonders to unfold in your life using life-giving words, and remember to use productive and empowering words. When people are mean or hurtful, it is natural to feel anger, but using simple words can help you maintain stability.

Saying "it's okay" acknowledges that people have their own opinions and judgments.

If you believe in God's judgment day, you will understand that you are not responsible for the words and actions of others. Instead, you will be accountable for how you react and your words.

If you don't believe in God's Judgment Day, why pass judgment on others? This doesn't mean we tolerate all forms of wrongdoing, but by saying, "It's okay," you can find stability in your mind and heart.

"No Problem" is another phrase that can help you maintain stability. If someone doesn't honor or greet you as they should, you can respond with "No Problem."

This phrase helps keep your mind and heart steady under challenging situations. Life-giving words are positive and straightforward words that bring calmness and stability.

By using the sentence "I know who I am," you establish a strong sense of self.

This statement is not meant to be arrogant but rather a reminder that you do not depend on validation from others. I recommend using this sentence only with those close to you, as others may not understand its meaning.

Let me share three more sentences that can anchor your mind and heart: "It's okay," "No Problem," and "I know who I am." These three sentences can be used in any situation.

When someone accuses you of being dishonest, you can respond with "It's okay for them to think what they are thinking, "No Problem" if they feel that I am not loyal or honest," and "I know who I am" - an honest and loyal person."

It is essential to regularly calm your mind and use these words to anchor yourself. Initially, it may be challenging, but with practice, you will master it.

These life-giving words anchor your mind and heart, allowing you to focus on your goals and move forward with purpose. Speaking life-giving words goes beyond simply using positive words.

The biggest mistake is using these words when your mind is not calm. Take the sentence "I know who I am" as an example. If your mind wanders due to emotions, using this sentence to justify yourself is not genuinely speaking life-giving words.

Life-giving words are transformative and have the power to bring about change. When you hear something unpleasant, the first step is to calm your mind; only then can you control your powerful tongue.

Once your mind is calm and you have control over your words, you can use the incredible power of life-giving words to uplift yourself and others.

Being cautious and using life-giving words is essential when surrounded by people who speak negatively.

Ultimately, they may have more influence due to their numbers and the energy they emit. However, you can still use subtle life-giving words. For example, you can say, "Why don't you try?" This is a gentle way of imparting life-giving words.

"I know you can do it "is another life-giving phrase. By expressing your belief in someone's abilities, you can gradually shift them away from negative energy and encourage productivity.

There are five more amazing powers of your tongue that you will learn about. If you read and apply the principles in this book to your life, you can succeed in any situation.

Wrapping Up

The key takeaway is clear: our words shape destinies. The chapter emphasizes the importance of consciously using life-giving words, providing practical phrases for anchoring the mind and heart.

By mastering this skill, the stage is set for success in any situation, paving the way for the exploration of five more incredible powers of the tongue in the upcoming chapters.

Chapter 3

The Incredible Power of Loving Words

The most important thing in life is

to learn how to give out Love,

and to let it come in -Mitch Albom

Synopsys

Enter the transformative realm of expressing love through the incredible power of our tongues in this enlightening chapter. Unlike previous discussions on life and death words, this segment explores the conscious decision to speak words of love, even when emotions may not align. Inspirational examples of individuals like Mr. Kalyansundram and Mother Teresa underscore the impact of deliberate acts of love. The chapter encourages readers to commit to spreading love through words in all circumstances, particularly within families.

Power of Loving Words

One of our tongue's most amazing powers is the ability to express love. In the previous chapters, we discussed how our words can bring either life or death. We can use our tongues to speak words that bring life and love into the world.

Before delving into the topic of using our tongues to express love, let's take a moment to talk about what love truly is. If you were to search for a definition of love, you would find countless interpretations. However, love is not merely a feeling or emotion but a conscious decision.

When we understand love as a decision, we can grasp the concept of speaking loving words even when we don't necessarily feel love in that moment.

In this chapter, we will explore how to utilize the power of our tongues to release words of love, even when we may not initially feel inclined to do so.

It's important to note that we will not be delving into the topic of unconditional love in this chapter. Explaining the depths of unconditional love in just one chapter would not do it justice, and even an entire book may not be sufficient to explore this vast subject fully.

Instead, this chapter focuses on using our tongues to speak words of love, even when we may not feel like talking. But before we delve into the specifics of this practice, let's take a moment to reflect on someone in your life who embodies love. I'm not referring to romantic or parental love but rather the love that emanates from individuals who genuinely care for others.

We can sense their passion, communication, gestures, and contributions when we encounter such individuals. While it may be challenging to come across such loving individuals in today's world, there are remarkable examples that inspire us.

For instance, Mr. Kalyansundram donated his entire salary as a librarian for 30 years. To meet his needs, he took up a job at a hotel. Kalyansundram received a prize of Rs 30 crore for his selfless actions, which he promptly gave to people experiencing poverty. When superstar Rajinikanth learned about this incredible act of kindness, he became Kalyansundram's fan and even adopted him as his father. Mr. Kalyansundram's contribution resulted from his conscious decision to help others.

Another remarkable example is Mother Teresa, born in Macedonia to Albanian parents and taught in India for 17 years. Mother Teresa discovered her calling in 1946 and founded centers for the blind, aged, and disabled, as well as a leper colony. By her passing in 1997, the Missionaries of Charity, the order she established, had grown to include over 4,000 members and thousands of lay volunteers, with 610 foundations in 123 countries worldwide. Mother Teresa's remarkable contributions were driven by her decision to show love and compassion.

I mention these extraordinary individuals to highlight the power of conscious decision-making in expressing love.

Love is not solely dependent on our emotions; it can be a deliberate choice. Imagine if we all consciously decided to show love, just as Mr. Kalyansundram and Mother Teresa did. Our planet would undoubtedly become a paradise.

Numerous philanthropists have made a significant impact on the lives of many. They choose to engage in acts of charity and contribute not solely based on their emotions but because they have consciously decided to do so.

Now, let us decide to use our tongues to release words of love. We must not limit ourselves to speaking loving words only when we feel good or positive emotions. We must commit to speaking words of love in all circumstances. This is the essence of this chapter.

You may have heard the proverb, "Charity begins at home." Let us apply this concept to our use of loving words.

Loving words with our children, spouses, and parents may be more accessible. Still, even these seemingly simple acts can be challenging due to the increasing conflicts, misunderstandings, irritations, and mental instability within families.

In this chapter, I will guide you on infusing your family with a loving vibration using the power of your words. Using your powerful tongue, you can begin to spread this
loving energy. However, before you embark on this journey, you must take one crucial step: decide to spread love in every situation and condition.

Whether you feel love or not or feel motivated or inspired, you must release words of love because you have consciously decided to do so.

There may be a majority of people around you who are negative, short-tempered, selfish, and egotistical, but you have decided to be a beacon of love. That is the most important thing.

Instead of discussing kind gestures and actions, this book focuses on the power of your words. We will explore using your tongue to spread love and positive energy.

When your words are filled with love, your heart can't be empty or cruel. As I explained in the previous chapter, your mouth speaks what your mind and heart feel. Even if your mind and heart are not filled with love, this chapter will teach you how to release loving words.

However, it is essential to exercise caution when using this technique. Suddenly, using loving words may seem strange to your loved ones. Be polite and use caring words such as "I know you need this" when offering or giving something. Always use soft words and express understanding before making suggestions. Remember, you must calm your mind to control your tongue.

Instead of constantly searching for flaws in everything, refrain from speaking with kindness and compassion towards others. This may not be easy to maintain for a long time, and if others respond similarly, you will feel satisfied. Start by speaking to yourself kindly and compassionately, then extend that love to others.

For example, if you lose something and start blaming yourself, slow down your thoughts and use your tongue to release the words slowly. Say to yourself, "Divine Love flows to me, and in the mind of infinite intelligence, there is no loss, so I lose nothing." Remember to calm your mind before speaking these loving words, even if you don't feel like doing so. Repeat this affirmation 10,000 times.

If someone is rude, slow down your thoughts and speak to yourself, saying, "I refuse to give power to any person, place, or thing to annoy me. I know that Infinite Intelligence resides within that person. They are filled with divine love, light, and truth." Even if you don't feel like releasing these loving words, you have decided to do so, and therefore, you must continue saying them.

In the event of a conflict with someone, slow down your thoughts and speak to yourself, saying, "I give thanks for the reconciliation that will happen at the perfect time and in a harmonious way. I release this person into the mighty hands of the All-wise One, the supreme God." Even if you don't feel like releasing these loving words, you have decided to do so, and therefore, you must continue saying them.

If you feel guilty, speak to yourself with kind and loving words. Using your tongue to release kind and loving words to yourself every moment, you can extend that kindness and love to others when you find them guilty and suffering.

Releasing loving words impacts your spirit, soul, and body. When you calm your mind and use your tongue to remove kind and compassionate words, you gain better control over your situations.

Your decision to release loving words holds great significance in all situations. If you allow yourself to be carried away by your feelings and emotions, you will fail to utilize the power of your tongue to spread loving vibrations within your family and your surroundings.

Your loving words have the power to change your life and the lives of others. So, don't hesitate to release caring and compassionate words from today onwards.

You can bring about the change you wish to see in your life, family, and world.

Congratulations on your commitment to releasing loving words in all situations, and I wish you all the best in becoming a new, loving person.

Wrapping Up

As we conclude this chapter on expressing love through our words, the central message resounds: love is not solely an emotion but a conscious decision. The remarkable stories shared inspire us to become beacons of love, like Mr. Kalyansundram and Mother Teresa.

The chapter guides readers on infusing family life with a loving vibration through deliberate words. A crucial takeaway is the commitment to release words of love, regardless of emotional states, understanding that this decision holds immense power to transform lives.

By harnessing the influence of the tongue, you embark on a journey to create positive change in yourself, your family, and the world. Congratulations on this commitment to becoming a source of love and positivity in all situations.

Chapter 4

The Incredible Power of Healing Words

Healing yourself is connected with

healing others- Yoko Ono

Synopsys

Discover the incredible power of healing words as we explore real-life stories from Argentina to Bangladesh. This chapter unravels the transformative impact of intentional language on physical, mental, and emotional well-being. Drawing on personal experiences, the narrative unveils the universal potential of the tongue in fostering healing. From restoring mobility to dispelling fear, the chapter offers a toolkit of healing words, empowering readers to embrace their transformative influence.

Power of Healing Words

The fourth incredible power that our tongue possesses is the power of healing.

Healing is a vital power that every individual requires. Allow me to recount a story about one of my friends from Argentina. We initially connected through an online platform, such as Facebook, although I am still trying to remember the exact one. After conversing for some time, she confided in me about her husband's inability to work due to an illness that rendered him unable to walk. Although I cannot recall the name of the disease she mentioned, she also shared that her children experienced fear at night, hindering their ability to sleep. As the sole provider for her family, she yearned for an improvement in her earnings but needed guidance about how to enhance her situation.

In response, I offered her guidance and provided her with healing words to repeat. I will also share a few of those words with you in this chapter. Whenever she reaches out to me to discuss her family's struggles, I offer her encouraging and healing words, along with various techniques.

Initially, she lacked confidence and struggled to comprehend English. However, over time, she grasped the essence of my message and began faithfully repeating the healing words, following my instructions.

Remarkably, within a few weeks, her husband began walking again, and the marks on his legs gradually disappeared (although I cannot verify the existence of these marks). I am merely relaying the information she shared with me.

She was overjoyed and filled with gratitude as her husband's ability to walk was restored after a year, and her children's night terrors ceased. Additionally, she gained a newfound sense of confidence and optimism. She expressed her gratitude to me countless times for the assistance

I provided. Even though I usually charge for my services, I did not accept any payment from her. However, she insisted on repaying me once she had sufficient funds. Such wonders happened in various people's lives from Argentina, Bangladesh, Pakistan, and other countries. I provided them with healing words, and they experienced remarkable healing.

Allow me to share another real-life incident involving a woman from a church where I used to preach and continue to do so online. One morning, she approached me in tears, informing me that her daughter was in the intensive care unit (ICU). The doctor had expressed pessimism regarding her daughter's chances of recovery due to the severity of her condition.

I inquired about the duration it took for her to travel from my location to the hospital. She mentioned that it typically took around 20-25 minutes by rickshaw. Without hesitation, I instructed her to repeat a specific word on her to the hospital, and when she arrived, she stood outside the ICU.

The word I shared with her was "Jesus, you are the resurrection and the life," as her faith resided in Jesus, and we often discussed biblical teachings. By referring to Jesus as the resurrection and the life, I aimed to remind her that Jesus had triumphed over death and was resurrected.

Almost two weeks later, this woman returned to the church and joyfully testified that her daughter's condition had significantly improved. This is a testament to the immense power of healing words that can be spoken using our powerful tongues.

I could continue sharing countless incidents and miracles highlighting the transformative effects of speaking healing words. The wonders that can be achieved through the power of our tongues are genuinely remarkable.

Allow me to recount an incident concerning my tongue that I experienced last year. Unexpectedly, I began to feel some discomfort in the front part of my tongue, which soon escalated into irritation and pain on both sides.

Despite undergoing various treatments, I found no relief. Filled with concern, I turned to the internet to research this peculiar condition, only to be met with fear that it might indicate a more serious underlying issue.

Seeking guidance, I contacted my trusted dentist, who advised me to seek immediate examination. Small blisters on the tongue can be excruciatingly painful, causing constant irritation.

Unaware of the cause behind my tongue's distress, I found myself plagued by this condition throughout the day, leaving me feeling disheartened.

Despite visiting numerous doctors, my efforts proved futile. Eventually, I decided to consult a specialist in mouth cancer. After securing an appointment, I patiently waited outside, anticipating my turn.

I sit in front of a highly recommended specialist in Mouth Cancer. The doctor carefully examined my tongue and suggested that it may be due to an allergy or a vitamin deficiency. Assuring me that it would improve, the doctor expressed surprise about why I came to them for such a minor issue.

Doctors sometimes understand our emotional state, and to ease my worried mind, the doctor prescribes a vitamin tablet and underlines the words "NOTHING TO WORRY" twice. This is the first time I have seen a doctor provide such reassurance in writing.

Typically, doctors don't simply say "NOTHING TO WORRY" without recommending further tests to rule out any underlying health conditions.

However, the doctor's written words carry a powerful healing message. We often underestimate the power of our words, especially regarding healing. Though small, our tongue can work miracles when we use it to speak healing words.

The connection between physical, mental, and emotional healing is closely tied to our tongue. Just as we place medication on our tongue before swallowing it, doctors use electronic thermometers under our tongues to check our body temperature.

We also use our tongues to pray for healing, recite healing affirmations, and chant mantras. Our tongues possess the potential to heal physical, mental, and emotional pain, but we must train ourselves to release healing words for both ourselves and others.

Creative Intelligence creates our bodies, and the Infinite Healing Presence knows how to restore and heal them.

The Infinite Intelligence within us controls our heart, mind, digestion, blood flow, and all other bodily functions. It guides our body's growth according to our age. The human body is marvelous, and we must continuously release healing words for perfect health.

Allow me to share a few healing words. When used meaningfully, these words can bring about positive changes in our physical, mental, and emotional well-being.

Forgiveness is a powerful healing word. Often, when we hear the word "forgiveness," our minds immediately think of forgiving others.

However, forgiveness is primarily about us. We tend to blame and hold guilt within ourselves, even if we are generous in forgiving others. We must release past mistakes and forgive both ourselves and others. This is the first step towards freedom and receiving healing.

If we still harbor anger, even if it is long-standing, it can block our healing power. We release the healing word of forgiveness by saying "I forgive you" to the person we are angry with, whether it's a family member or anyone else.

Forgiving ourselves is equally important. If we have done something wrong or carry guilt for losing something valuable, we must release the words "I forgive you" followed by our name.

We should stop blaming ourselves and refrain from unnecessary self-punishment. We must remember that we have always done our best.

Peace begins with us, a healing word that signifies the absence of war and disturbance and the presence of harmony and tranquility. By releasing the healing words "Peace begins with me," we become the catalyst for peace and harmony. We can end conflicts and create a calm and peaceful environment.

Even when we feel weak, we can use the healing words "I am strong" to change our lives positively. It is astonishing how our words can influence our state of being. We can witness the wonders it brings into our lives by repeatedly saying, "I am strong," even if we don't feel it initially.

While I cannot delve into the details of these healing words in this book, I am open to discussing them further if you contact me. I can help you understand the psychological effects of releasing healing words.

Another powerful healing statement is, "I permit myself to be healed." Humans tend to worry even when there is nothing to worry about.

This worrying nature obstructs our healing process. By releasing the healing words "I permit myself to be healed" when worry strikes, we open ourselves up to physical, mental, and emotional healing.

If past traumas continue to haunt us, we can use our tongues to release healing words. Patients need to cooperate with doctors during treatment.

While doctors can prescribe medication, we must take it and allow our bodies to respond positively. We enhance the healing process by taking medicine and simultaneously releasing healing words.

"I am getting better and better every day" is another healing word that has brought about positive transformations in countless lives. We invite continuous improvement and better outcomes into our lives by repeating this healing statement seven times before starting our day and falling asleep.

Healing words are meant for ourselves and can be given to others.

However, possessing a powerful and energetic aura before sharing these words is crucial. Meditation and strong faith in the Divine can help maintain this aura.

Healers, monks, church leaders, and saints possess this power and use it to bring faith and healing to others through their words. Before giving healing words to others, we must develop a strong aura and speak with trust and confidence. Over time, we can align ourselves with the healing energy.

To align ourselves with the Divine Healing Power, we must know it resides within everyone. We can heal ourselves and others by releasing healing words with this knowledge.

We must utilize the power of our tongues to release healing words instead of harmful ones. By using our tongues to speak healing words, we can bring about a transformation in our own lives and the lives of those around us.

It would help if you started using these simple healing words within your family and then extended them to others.

Words such as "You will be alright soon," "I know you will recover quickly," "She/He will be alright," and "I prayed for your healing" can make a significant difference.

Remember, there is nothing to worry about, and the Infinite Healing Power is at work. Visualize the person getting better each day and affirm their strength, good immunity, and imminent recovery.

You can bring healing to yourself and others through the power of your words.

Best wishes for your healing journey.

Wrapping Up

As we conclude this enlightening chapter, let the stories inspire you to wield the power of healing words. Whether for personal challenges or extending healing to others, remember that your tongue holds a remarkable force for positive change.

May the shared experiences motivate you on your healing journey, using simple yet impactful words to shape a healthier and happier life.

Best wishes as you explore the transformative potential within your own words.

= = = = = = = = = = = = = = = = = =

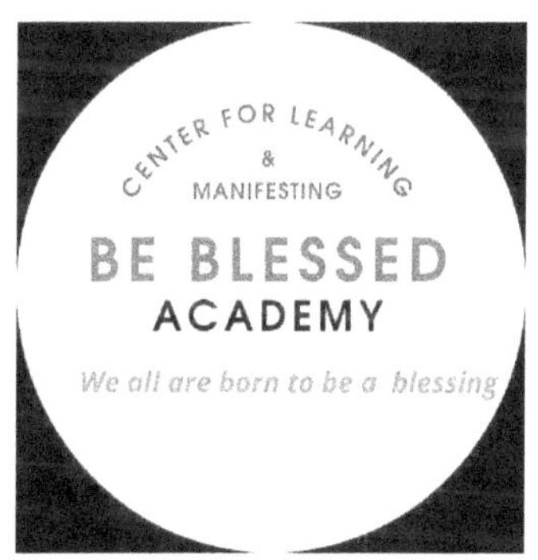

Chapter 5

The Incredible Power of Rich Words

True wealth is not of the pocket, but of the

Heart and of the mind-Kevin Gates

Synopsys

Unlock the transformative potential of words in the pursuit of wealth. Delve into the story of Alexander and Thomas, contrasting views on riches, and their journey towards a harmonious balance. Discover the profound impact of language on financial success and explore the essence of daily affirmations to attract abundance. This chapter unravels the intricate connection between spoken words and financial well-being, guiding readers to embrace positivity and reshape their financial narratives.

Power of Rich Words

A verse in the Bible holds immense power: "God Gives the Power to get wealth." This verse has completely transformed my perspective on wealth acquisition. I delved deep into understanding how God grants power and discovered that our words hold tremendous power.

Our words can either uplift us or bring us down. We invite wealth into our lives by using our tongues to speak words of abundance and prosperity.

In today's complex world, even the most ordinary individuals require significant wealth to live fulfilling lives.

Let me share a tale of two men, Alexander and Thomas, who had contrasting views on wealth. Alexander, a prosperous and ambitious man, believed that material possessions and riches were the keys to happiness. On the other hand, Thomas believed in finding contentment in life's simple pleasures and eschewed the pursuit of abundance.

Alexander and Thomas crossed paths one fateful day and engaged in a thought-provoking conversation. Alexander passionately argued that the desire for riches was natural and commendable, as it drove individuals to achieve greatness and provide for their loved ones. Thomas, however, calmly shared his belief that true happiness couldn't be measured by the size of one's bank account. He emphasized the importance of finding joy in simple pleasures and meaningful relationships.

As the sun set and bathed the village in a golden glow, Alexander and Thomas realized their perspectives were not as incompatible as they initially thought. Alexander recognized that his pursuit of wealth had come at a cost - he had sacrificed precious moments and neglected his well-being. On the other hand, Thomas acknowledged that his aversion to wealth had limited his potential for growth and impact.
At that moment, they found common ground. They understood that when balanced with

gratitude and a sense of purpose, the desire for riches could lead to a life of abundance and fulfillment. They both agreed that wealth should be defined not only in monetary terms but also in terms of experiences, relationships, and personal growth.

From that day forward, Alexander and Thomas embarked on a new journey together. They sought harmony between their desires for wealth and contentment, understanding that true prosperity lay in finding balance and living a life aligned with their values.

This story serves as a reminder to all of us. When tempered with wisdom and a generous spirit, the desire for riches can lead to a life of abundance and fulfillment.

It is not abnormal to aspire to the comforts that money can bring, but it is equally important to appreciate life's simple joys each day.

So, let us embrace the desire for riches with open hearts and minds. Let us not shy away from our dreams of abundance, for they are a testament to our unwavering spirit and belief in the infinite possibilities that lie before us.

As we embark on this extraordinary journey, let us remember that the pursuit of riches is not a solitary endeavor but a collective endeavor that encompasses the hopes and dreams of all humanity.

We can speak words of abundance and prosperity into our lives. However, it is essential to acknowledge that it may be challenging for those in middle or lower-class situations to release rich words due to their circumstances.

Those below the poverty line must undergo a transformative experience and understand the concept of speaking rich words.

Releasing rich words can bring wonders into our lives, but it must become a daily practice to change how we speak. If we don't change our speaking patterns, we won't be able to change our financial circumstances.

The power lies in our tongues. We will witness miracles when we speak rich words with our powerful tongues.

As human beings, we often prioritize taking action. However, it is essential to recognize that our chosen words are just as significant as our actions.

Let me provide an example to illustrate this point. When someone we care about expresses their feelings, our immediate response may be to offer solutions and advice. However, sometimes, what they truly need is our presence, support, and active listening.

Actions are necessary, but the right words give us the right direction to take action.

When acquiring wealth, it is crucial to understand that we must speak the right and rich words to pave the way for financial success.

You may have heard and even affirmed statements like "I am wealthy" and "I am rich." While these affirmations are beneficial, it is essential to note that merely saying these words for a few minutes in the morning will not override the negative words we speak throughout the day.

It is essential to consistently speak words of abundance and prosperity to align our financial vibration and attract wealth into our lives.

This chapter will explore incorporating positive affirmations into our daily lives to attract wealth and abundance.

One powerful affirmation you can start with is, "I love Money, and Money loves me." It is expected to associate loving money with greed or evil, but the truth is we all desire and need money in our lives.

By acknowledging and embracing our love for money, we open ourselves up to receiving it. Money is like a beautiful feminine energy that needs our love and appreciation. When we genuinely love money, it reciprocates that love back to us.

It is essential to stop criticizing and judging others who have money. When we do this, we charge wealth itself, which hinders our ability to attract it. Instead, we should focus on releasing positive and empowering statements like "I love Money and Money loves me."

Another powerful affirmation is "I can afford it." Instead of saying something is too expensive or can't buy it, we should affirm that we can afford it. By confidently stating, "I can afford it," we align ourselves with the universe's abundant possibilities and open ourselves up to receiving what we desire.

We often underestimate our worthiness to live a life of abundance. Many believe they are unworthy due to cultural, environmental, or genetic factors. This belief of unworthiness blocks the flow of abundance in their lives. However, we must recognize that we all deserve divine blessings, support, and healing.

By affirming "I know I am worthy," we allow ourselves to receive the abundance that is rightfully ours.

We tend to believe that bad things can happen to us quickly but struggle to believe that good things can come our way.

This is due to the negative mass consciousness that surrounds us. However, by affirming "I know good things are coming my way," we shift our mindset and open ourselves up to the positive possibilities that the universe has in store for us.

Passion is a critical ingredient in attracting wealth. Many people settle for contentment, but wealthy individuals are driven by their passion for wealth. By affirming "I am passionate about wealth," we ignite a fire within ourselves that attracts opportunities and ideas for wealth creation.

A common belief is that getting money is hard, and this belief becomes our reality. However, we can change this by believing in the easy flow of money.

By affirming "Money flows to me easily," we shift our mindset and allow abundance to come into our lives effortlessly.

When we consistently release these rich statements and genuinely believe in them, we open ourselves to a world of possibilities.

Ideas, opportunities, and like-minded individuals will come into our lives, making our journey towards wealth and abundance easier.

Divine guidance will lead us in the right direction, and money will flow effortlessly.

By harnessing the power of our tongue and incorporating these positive affirmations into our daily lives, we can attract abundance and release the limitations of scarcity.

Let us embrace the truth of our worthiness and the easy flow of money and watch as our lives transform into ones filled with wealth and prosperity.

God Gives Power to Get

Wrapping Up

As we conclude this chapter, remember the remarkable influence your words wield in the realm of wealth. The tale of Alexander and Thomas serves as a testament to the delicate balance needed in our pursuit of abundance.

Daily affirmations act as a beacon, guiding us toward a mindset of prosperity. Embrace the power of positive language, affirm your worthiness, and believe in the effortless flow of money.

Your tongue holds the key to unlocking a life filled with wealth and prosperity. May your journey be adorned with financial abundance and transformative words.

Chapter 6

The Incredible Power of Appreciating Words

Don't forget, a person's greatest emotional need is to feel appreciated- H. Jackson Brown Jr.

Synopsys

Dive into the transformative power of appreciation, the sixth incredible ability of your tongue. In a world filled with criticism, discover how sincere words of gratitude act as a sweet tonic, soothing the spirit. The chapter unfolds the profound impact of genuine appreciation on relationships, emphasizing its role in building strong foundations and boosting productivity.

Power of Appreciating Words

The Sixth Incredible Power of Your Tongue is the ability to express words of appreciation.

Appreciation is the opposite of depreciation, which means to undervalue or criticize.

Unfortunately, we often hear more criticism than appreciation in today's world. Personal and business gossip often revolves around putting others down.

Even on the news, debates are filled with depreciating remarks. While we can't change the world, we can start by changing ourselves and our families.

Sincere words of appreciation have a sweet and soothing effect. They are like honey for the body.

Wives seek appreciation from their husbands, and vice versa. Children long for their parents' appreciation. Employees crave recognition from their bosses. Appreciation is a healthy tonic, but our society is filled with fault-finding and criticism.

We must educate and train people to speak words of appreciation as much as possible. Genuine appreciation has the power to uplift spirits.

Let's consider an example: if a wife consistently expresses her gratitude to her husband every morning before he leaves for work, saying, "I truly appreciate the hard work you do for me, our children, and our family," imagine the impact it would have on him. I guarantee that he would carry those kind words with him throughout the day, perhaps even smiling and singing a joyful tune on his way. Sadly, many wives blame and criticize their hard-working husbands instead of appreciating them for keeping the family happy and healthy.

For a wife to appreciate her husband daily requires a deep love for him. Love can overlook faults and see a person for who they indeed are. When you are in love, you accept and cherish your partner as they are and make the commitment to spend the rest of your life with them. However, when the love begins to fade, it becomes easier to focus on the negative aspects of your partner, leading to a decrease in appreciation.

You naturally notice and acknowledge their positive qualities when you genuinely love someone. You express words of appreciation that strengthen the relationship. You appreciate their sense of style, smile, way of speaking, and thoughts. This mutual appreciation builds a strong foundation for the relationship.

It is important to note that we are not entirely to blame for our lack of appreciation. As I mentioned earlier, we become what we constantly hear. We tend to adopt the same behavior if regularly exposed to criticism.

Our family, mainly our parents, greatly influences our communication habits. If we do not receive words of appreciation from our parents, we may seek it from others. This is why some children are particularly attached to their grandparents, as they often provide the appreciative words they crave.

Sometimes, we may feel more connected to a favorite aunt or uncle than our parents because they do not depreciate us as our parents or siblings might. We all need appreciation, as it serves as a daily motivator to become more efficient. Wherever there is sincere appreciation, there is always high productivity.

Throughout this chapter, I have emphasized the importance of sincere appreciation. There are many instances where we encounter fake or insincere appreciation, comparable to dark clouds that disappear once the rain is over. I encourage you always to express genuine and sincere appreciation. If you need help with how to do so, continue reading this chapter, as I will share some valuable insights that will assist you.

It is important to note that phrases such as "you are looking smart," "you are handsome," "you are looking pretty," and "you are dynamic" are not genuine expressions of appreciation.

Sincere and genuine appreciation is appreciating that person's good character, ability, determination, dedication, and nature.

To appreciate a person sincerely and genuinely, you should know that person well. You are not just enjoying the outer appearance but respecting the whole person.

In a world where genuine appreciation was a rare gem, there lived a wise individual who understood the true essence of appreciating others. This person knew that to enjoy someone truly, one must delve deep into their soul and understand every facet of their being. It was not enough to merely admire their outer appearance; genuine appreciation required a profound understanding of the whole person.

In relationships, this wise individual knew that expressing heartfelt appreciation to their spouse went beyond surface-level compliments. When they turned to their beloved wife and said, "I appreciate your unwavering care and concern for my family and me," it was a genuine expression of gratitude. He recognized the strength and determination within his wife and made sure to acknowledge it, saying, "I appreciate your resilience and the fact that you are a strong woman."

Likewise, when it came to their mother, this wise individual knew that genuine appreciation meant recognizing her nurturing nature. With a warm smile, they would say, "Mom, I appreciate your boundless love and care." It was a heartfelt acknowledgment of their mother's countless sacrifices.

But what about appreciating a man? This wise individual knew that sincere and honest appreciation for a man came from observing him closely. When he turned to a man and said, "You are a good-hearted and hard-working individual," it was a genuine expression of admiration. He had taken the time to understand the man's character and recognized his sincerity and dedication.

And when it came to the ultimate appreciation, this wise individual knew that knowing a person's heart was no easy task. Yet, when he looked at a man and said, "You are good-looking with a good heart," it was a sincere and genuine appreciation. It was a testament to their deep understanding of the man's true nature.

This wise individual sought clarity in a world where flattery often disguised itself as appreciation. He understood that sincere and genuine appreciation was not merely a few words thrown around lightly. It was a reward for the person who received such appreciation and recognition of their true worth.

So, my dear readers, let us learn from this wise individual's example. Let us strive to know and understand those we appreciate genuinely.

Let us express our gratitude in a way that goes beyond the surface, for it is in genuine appreciation that authentic connections are forged and hearts are touched.

Wrapping Up

As we conclude, envision a wise individual navigating a world where flattery masks itself as appreciation. Learn from their example, understanding that genuine appreciation transcends surface-level compliments.

It delves deep into a person's character, recognizing their strength, determination, and true nature. Let this wisdom guide us to express heartfelt gratitude, forging authentic connections and touching hearts in the process. May the sincerity of our appreciation echo in the hearts of those we cherish.

Chapter 7

The Incredible Power of Words of Wisdom

Knowledge knows that a tomato is a fruit; wisdom is not putting it in a fruit salad -Miles Kington

Synopsys

Uncover the sixth incredible power of the human tongue – the ability to express words of wisdom. This chapter delves into the distinction between foolishness and wisdom, emphasizing the importance of thoughtful listening and the art of imparting wisdom through engaging narratives. The wise person in this chapter shares valuable insights on how to effectively communicate wisdom, blending authority, storytelling, and inspiration to leave an enduring impact.

Power of Words of Wisdom

The seventh incredible power of the human tongue lies in its ability to express words of wisdom.

It is said that a foolish individual is quick to start a fight, quickly gets upset, and enjoys talking but despises listening.

We can determine whether we are releasing foolishness or wisdom into the world through the words we choose to speak.

Wisdom goes beyond simply sharing knowledge. It is rooted in personal experiences, not just accumulated information.

Knowledge is what we know, but wisdom measures how wise we are. If we lack intelligence, then we are considered fools.

However, if we possess wisdom, we are regarded as wise individuals. Wise people utilize their knowledge thoughtfully. Many individuals may know but need more wisdom to apply it effectively.

In this chapter, I will delve into expressing words of wisdom. The first quality that distinguishes a wise person is their ability to listen attentively.

Fools dominate conversations, often without a deep understanding of the subject matter. Conversely, wise individuals prioritize listening over speaking, recognizing the value of gaining knowledge through attentive listening.

In a world filled with seekers of wisdom, there lived a wise person who possessed a unique understanding of the power of listening. This sage knew that actual knowledge could only be imparted after careful and attentive listening, allowing the words of wisdom to flow effortlessly from their lips.

In this bustling world, the wise person understood the importance of brevity, much like a doctor prescribing a treatment plan to a patient. They recognized that not everyone could comprehend the complexities of their wisdom. Therefore, they chose to share only a few select words, refraining from overwhelming their listeners with abundant information.

However, the challenge lay in conveying this wisdom to loved ones, such as spouses or grown-up children. The wise person knew that speaking words of wisdom to those closest to them required a delicate approach. They understood it was akin to hitting their head against a wall when attempting to enlighten a fool. Thus, they employed the art of storytelling, weaving their wisdom into captivating tales.

Imagine a scenario where a person finds themselves drowning in a sea of debt. The wise person recognizes an opportunity to offer valuable advice, knowing full well that the individual may need to be more receptive to it. They would craft a fictional narrative in such instances, subtly embedding their sage counsel within the story. By doing so, the listener would not perceive the wise person's intentions as an attempt to impose their wisdom but rather as an engaging tale with a valuable lesson.

For those who lacked the skill to construct a compelling narrative, the wise person recommended attributing the wisdom to a renowned figure, such as a Guru, Maharaj, or Mentor. By presenting the advice as originating from a respected authority, they minimized the chances of facing mockery or being held accountable if the advice did not yield the desired outcome.

In this world, people were conditioned to believe that only those in positions of authority possessed the ability to dispense wisdom. Thus, the wise person understood the importance of creating an authoritative persona to share their insights. By assuming this role, they shielded themselves from direct criticism and avoided being burdened with responsibility if their wisdom did not bear fruit.

And so, the wise person continued their journey, sharing their wisdom through carefully crafted stories and imaginative narratives. They understood that actual knowledge was not about asserting authority but connecting with others and guiding them toward enlightenment. In this way, they left an indelible mark on the hearts and minds of all who crossed their path, forever inspiring others to seek wisdom in the most unexpected places.

Unlock the potential of your voice to share valuable insights, whether through personal anecdotes, fictional tales, or by drawing inspiration from influential figures. Your life experiences hold a wealth of wisdom, but if you need more in this area, you can actively seek knowledge to enrich your mind. Remember, wisdom goes beyond mere knowledge; it is practical and can be acquired by studying the triumphs and challenges faced by real-life champions. Engaging with books and articles that delve into these experiences will help you fill your mind with wisdom.

When communicating with your family, it is essential to adopt an authoritative persona to convey your wise advice effectively. Your spouse and children may not readily view you as intelligent, but presenting your wisdom as if this classic figure shares it may make them more inclined to listen.

Think back to the story of the wise man that approached the hunchback king, requesting him to straighten a statue. This tale serves as a clear example of imparting wisdom. The wise man respectfully sought the king's input before sharing his advice, understanding that directly addressing a king can be offensive and disrespectful. The fact that the king listened demonstrates his wisdom.

Refrain from disheartening if people fail to heed your words of wisdom. Recognizing that fools often love to talk but hate to listen is crucial. A wise person imparts their wisdom with politeness. We must all strive to master the art of speaking politely, but it is worth noting that our communication habits greatly influence our speech patterns.

We possess the power to impart words of wisdom. We must refrain from foolishly engaging in fights, arguments, unhealthy debates, criticism, and unnecessary comments.

Let us be wise fathers, mothers, husbands, wives, sons, daughters, brothers, sisters, employees, employers, neighbors, and citizens. Whenever you feel the urge to speak foolishly, exercise restraint by keeping your mind calm; when your mind is at peace, you can control your tongue, as it is intricately connected to your thoughts.

While many attempt to control their speech, it is only possible when they gain control over their minds. By monitoring the waves of our thoughts, we can safeguard our tongues.

The power of our tongues is genuinely remarkable, possessing the ability to bring life and death, love and hate, healing and disease, wealth and poverty, appreciation and deprecation, and wisdom and foolishness.

Choose to speak life instead of death, love instead of hate, healing instead of disease, wealth instead of poverty, appreciation instead of deprecation, and wisdom instead of foolishness.

Harness the power of your tongue to release life, love, healing, health, appreciation and wisdom.

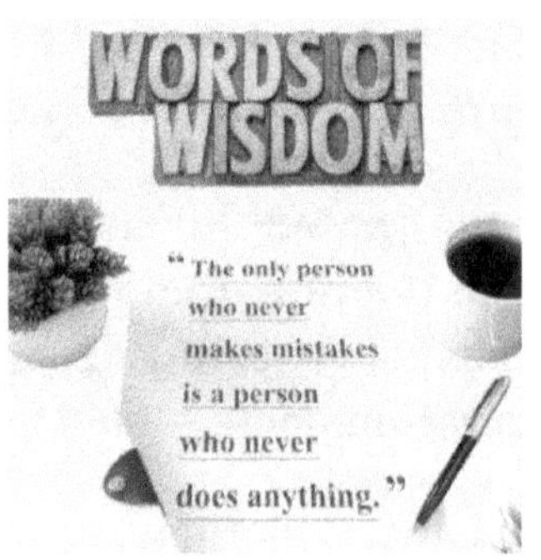

Wrapping Up

As we conclude this chapter, envision the transformative potential of your voice to share wisdom. Whether through personal anecdotes, fictional tales, or drawing inspiration from influential figures, your words can guide and enlighten.

Recognize the importance of presenting wisdom with authority, engaging your family and others respectfully.

Remember the tale of the wise man approaching the hunchback king, showcasing the art of imparting wisdom with humility. Strive to speak politely, refraining from engaging in futile arguments or criticism. Let your tongue be a source of life, love, healing, wealth, appreciation, and wisdom, harnessing its remarkable power to shape a positive and enlightened world.

Namaste and welcome to the transformative experience of our "Feel It and Achieve It" workshops – a unique and empowering journey rooted in the profoundprinciples of the Law of Assumption. This workshop is designed to help you manifest your desires with ease and speed, offering a variety of techniques to boost productivity and foster success.

Our workshops draw inspiration from the Law of Assumption, providing a fresh perspective that goes beyond the commonly discussed Law of Attraction. We guide you to assume the reality of your desires, tapping into your inner power to shape your destiny with intention and confidence.

Throughout these engaging sessions, we share a toolkit of proven techniques, including the art of visualization and the science of affirmations. These practices are tailored to provide a comprehensive approach to manifestation, ensuring you not only feel the resonance of your desires but also take practical steps towards turning them into reality.

Get ready to witness a shift in your mindset as you explore the core principles of assumption and manifestation. Our workshops create an atmosphere of growth, productivity, and abundance, guiding you to unlock your untapped potential and move towards a life filled with success and fulfillment.

Join us on this empowering journey, where your understanding of the Law of Assumption becomes the key to a life where your dreams are not just imagined but felt, embraced, and ultimately achieved. Swagat hai aapka - "Feel It and Achieve It" mein, jahan aapke gehre iraadon aur assumption ke shakti se nayi zindagi ki shuruaat hoti hai.

Mindful Living Unleashed: Harnessing the Power of Self-Discovery,
Spiritual Enlightment and Positive Transformation

ONLINE

BE BLESSED ACADEMY

JOHN BAPTIST NATHAN

BE BLESSED ACADEMY, YOUR ONLINE HAVEN FOR SELF-DEVELOPMENT AND BIBLICAL TEACHINGS!

DIVE INTO A TRANSFORMATIVE JOURNEY WHERE ANCIENT WISDOM MEETS MODERN GROWTH STRATEGIES.

JOIN OUR COMMUNITY COMMITTED TO PERSONAL EMPOWERMENT AND SPIRITUAL ENRICHMENT.

CONNECT WITH US ON SOCIAL MEDIA:
INSTAGRAM: BLESSEDCOMMUNITY2021

FOR COLLABORATION OR INQUIRIES, REACH OUT AT
[BEBLESSEDACADEMY@GMAIL.COM]

DON'T MISS OUR ENLIGHTENING VIDEOS - SUBSCRIBE NOW!

EVERY UPLOAD IS A BLEND OF PRACTICAL SELF-DEVELOPMENT TIPS AND PROFOUND BIBLICAL INSIGHTS.

EXPLORE THE PATH TO A BLESSED LIFE THROUGH OUR UNIQUE PERSPECTIVE.

READY TO TRANSFORM YOUR LIFE?

CLICK SUBSCRIBE, HIT THE NOTIFICATION BELL, AND EMBARK ON A JOURNEY TOWARDS A MORE ENLIGHTENED AND EMPOWERED YOU.

BE BLESSED, BE EMPOWERED!